W9-BDW-468

NOCK-KNOCK!
        WHO'S THERE?
YULE!
        YULE **WHO?**
**YULE LOVE THE MIGHTY BIG
BOOK OF KNOCK-KNOCKS!**

MIGHTY BIG
BOOK OF
KNOCK,
KNOCK!
JOKES!

LIBRARY O' LAUGHS

DEDICATED
to
CLIZKA
YOU BRING ME
MORE JOY
THAN ALL THE
JOKES IN THE
WORLD!

COPYRIGHT © 2002 BY CRAIG YOE. ILLUSTRATIONS COPYRIGHT © 2002 BY CRAIG YOE.
ALL RIGHTS RESERVED. PUBLISHED BY PRICE STERN SLOAN, A DIVISION OF PENGUIN
PUTNAM BOOKS FOR YOUNG READERS, 345 HUDSON STREET, NEW YORK, NY 10014.
PRINTED IN THE UNITED STATES OF AMERICA. PUBLISHED SIMULTANEOUSLY IN CANADA.
NO PART OF THIS PUBLICATION MAY BE REPRODUCED, STORED IN ANY RETRIEVAL SYSTEM
OR TRANSMITTED, IN ANY FORM OR BY ANY MEANS, ELECTRONIC, MECHANICAL,
PHOTOCOPYING, RECORDING, OR OTHERWISE, WITHOUT THE WRITTEN
PERMISSION OF THE PUBLISHER.

LIBRARY OF CONGRESS CATALOGING-IN-PUBLICATION DATA IS AVAILABLE.

ISBN 0-8431-7735-7
C D E F G H I J

PSS! IS A REGISTERED TRADEMARK OF PENGUIN PUTNAM INC.

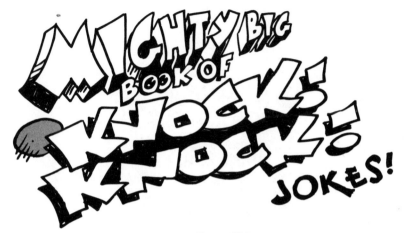

MIGHTY BIG BOOK OF KNOCK! KNOCK! JOKES!

by CRAIG YOE

WEBMASTER OF
WWW.RIDDLES4KIDS.COM

CO-WRITTEN BY
PATRICIA PASQUALE

LIBRARY O' LAUGHS

PSS!
PRICE STERN SLOAN

**NOCK-KNOCK!**
WHO'S THERE?
THANK!
THANK **WHO?**
THANK YOU!
CLIZIA GUSSONI (THE **GREAT DESIGNER** OF
THIS BOOK), **PATRICIA PASQUALE,**
JAYNE ANTIPOW, JON ANDERSON,
KELLI CHIPPONERI, AND **KAREN FINKEL** FOR THE
SUPPORT AND UNBOUNDED CREATIVITY YOU
DONATED TO THIS PROJECT. THANK YOU
ROSALIE LENT FOR THE THANK YOU PAGE IDEA.

CLIZIA WOULD ALSO LIKE TO THANK HER **FAMILY**
AND **FRIENDS** WHO APPEAR IN MANY OF THE
PHOTOS FOR THE **GRACE** WITH WHICH THEY LET
HER MOCK THEM.

**Door Knobbies!**
What do you say when a hot dog
opens the door for you?
"Franks a lot!"

KNOCK-KNOCK!
WHO'S **THERE**, YOU ASK?
NOBODY. IT'S JUST **ME.**

SORRY ABOUT THAT, BUT AFTER WRITING **ALL** THE **JOKES** IN THIS **BOOK,** I SEEM TO START **ALL** MY SENTENCES WITH **"KNOCK-KNOCK"** NOW. BUT THAT'S **OK! SO WHAT** IF PEOPLE LOOK AT ME **FUNNY** AT THE **DRIVE-THRU** WHEN I SAY, **"KNOCK-KNOCK, I'D LIKE FRIES WITH THAT!"** AND **BIG WHOOP** THAT I GET **STARES** AT **PARTIES** WHEN I SAY **"KNOCK-KNOCK, WOULD YOU LIKE TO DANCE?"** AS LONG AS THIS **BOOK** MAKES YOU **LAUGH,** THEN IT'S **ALL WORTH IT!**

YOUR PAL,

CRAIG

CRAIG **WHO?**

OH, NO... THIS IS GETTING **MUCH** WORSE...

KNOCK-KNOCK!

WHO'S THERE?

DOUGHNUT!

DOUGHNUT WHO?

DOUGHNUT YOU WANNA OPEN THE DOOR AND FIND OUT?

KNOCK-KNOCK!
WHO'S THERE?
EMMA!
EMMA **WHO?**
EMMA GONNA HAVE TO **KNOCK AGAIN,** OR ARE YOU GONNA **OPEN** THIS **DOOR?**

What number is on Tiger Woods' front door?
Fore!

KNOCK-KNOCK!
    WHO'S THERE?
MIKEY!
        MIKEY **WHO?**
MIKEY IS IN MY OTHER **PANTS!**

KNOCK-KNOCK!
WHO'S THERE?
LUKE!
LUKE **WHO?**
LUKE THROUGH THE **PEEPHOLE**
AND **FIND OUT!**

KNOCK-KNOCK!

WHO'S THERE?

CARRIE!

CARRIE WHO?

CARRIE THESE GROCERIES IN FOR ME, WILL YA?

KNOCK-KNOCK!
WHO'S THERE?
ALEXA!
ALEXA WHO?
ALEXA TO OPEN THE DOOR JUST ONE MORE TIME!

Answer The Door!

What do you wipe your feet on at a dog lover's house? *A mutt!*

CAN YOU GET THAT?

What do you use to open the
door at Thanksgiving?
A tur-key!

KNOCK-KNOCK!
WHO'S THERE?
LAURA!
LAURA **WHO?**
LAURA THE BLINDS,
I CAN **SEE** YOU!

 **KNOCK-KNOCK!**
WHO'S THERE?
RILEY!
RILEY **WHO?**
RILEY NOW, YOU MUST **KNOW**
WHO I AM!

KNOCK-KNOCK!
WHO'S THERE?
ALEXIS!
ALEXIS **WHO?**
ALEXIS IS BLOCKING MY CAR IN; IS IT YOURS?

KNOCK-KNOCK! Who's There?

ASHLEY!

ASHLEY WHO?

ASHLEY, IT'S NONE OF YOUR BUSINESS!

 NOCK-KNOCK!
WHO'S THERE?
SARA!
SARA WHO?
SARA DOCTOR IN THE HOUSE?

KNOCK-KNOCK!

WHO'S THERE?

CZAR!

CZAR **WHO?**

CZAR'S GOLD IN THEM THAR **HILLS!**

YOE!

DOOR SLAMS!

What number is on a ballerina's front door?
2-2!

KNOCK-KNOCK!
WHO'S THERE?
ALEX!
ALEX **WHO?**
ALEX-IT HERE -- OR IS **THIS**
THE **ENTRANCE?**

KNOCK-KNOCK!

WHO'S THERE?

PHILIP!

PHILIP **WHO?**

PHILIP THE **CANDY DISH,** I'VE GOT
A **SWEET TOOTH!**

KNOCK-KNOCK!
WHO'S THERE?
ANNIE!
ANNIE **WHO?**
ANNIE REASON IN PARTICULAR
YOU'RE **NOT** LETTING ME **IN?**

KNOCK-KNOCK!
WHO'S THERE?
LETTUCE!
LETTUCE WHO?
LETTUCE IN AND YOU'LL FIND OUT!

Door Knobbies!

What sign will you find on a
vacationing plumber's door?
Gone flushing!

KNOCK-KNOCK!
    WHO'S THERE?
OLIVE!
        OLIVE **WHO?**
OLIVE NEXT DOOR -- JUST
WANTED TO SAY **HI!**

KNOCK-KNOCK!

WHO'S THERE?

ADAIR!

ADAIR **WHO?**

ADAIR YOU TO FIND OUT!

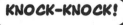

KNOCK-KNOCK!

WHO'S THERE?

ALLISON!

ALLISON **WHO?**

ALLISON HERE-- YOU LET ME IN!

KNOCK-KNOCK!

WHO'S THERE?

ALFONSO!

ALFONSO **WHO?**

ALFONSO YOU'LL KNOW I'M **ON MY WAY** NEXT TIME!

KNOCK-KNOCK!
WHO'S THERE?
ARCH!
ARCH **WHO?**
ARCH-N'T YOU GONNA **LET ME IN?**

KNOCK-KNOCK! WHO'S THERE?

ARETHA!

ARETHA **WHO?**

ARETHA IS HANGING ON MY **DOOR-A!**

JOE!

RNOCK-KNOCK!
WHO'S THERE?
ARVID!
ARVID **WHO?**
ARVID-EOS ARE **OVERDUE!**

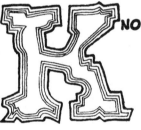NOCK-KNOCK!
   WHO'S THERE?
DON!
   DON **WHO?**
DON BE SILLY--
YOU **KNOW**
WHO IT IS!

 Ding Dong!

**What kind of door does a
sleeping person have?**
A snore door!

KNOCK-KNOCK!
 WHO'S THERE?
BECK!
 BECK **WHO?**
BECK OFF, WILL YA?

KNOCK-KNOCK!

WHO'S THERE?

AMARILLO!

AMARILLO **WHO?**

AMARILLO TIMER!

KNOCK-KNOCK!

Who's There?

BENJAMIN!

BENJAMIN **WHO?**

BENJAMIN ON MY GUITAR OUT HERE -- WHAT DO YOU THINK?!

KNOCK-KNOCK!
  WHO'S THERE?
BERN!
  BERN **WHO?**
BERN DINNER? IT SMELLS OUT HERE!

KNOCK-KNOCK!
WHO'S THERE?
CAESAR!
CAESAR WHO?
CAESARS HELP YOU CUT THINGS!

KNOCK-KNOCK!
WHO'S THERE?
CARGO!
CARGO WHO?
CARGO "VROOM VROOM!"

Door Knobbies!

What kind of door do you find at a
beach house?
A shore door!

KNOCK KNOCK!
WHO'S THERE?

CHANTEL!

CHANTEL WHO?

CHANTEL YA, SORRY!

KNOCK-KNOCK!
   WHO'S THERE?
CAROLYN!
   CAROLYN WHO?
CHRISTMAS CAROLYN!

I-Screen, You-Screen!

What kind of door does a basketball player have?
A score door!

 NOCK-KNOCK!
WHO'S THERE?
SISSY!
SISSY WHO?
SISSY RIGHT HOUSE?

**NOCK-KNOCK!**
WHO'S THERE?
DUNCAN!
DUNCAN **WHO?**
DUNCAN YO-YO!

KNOCK-KNOCK!
WHO'S THERE?
WALTER!
WALTER **WHO?**
WALTER OFF A DUCK'S BACK!

NOCK-KNOCK!
WHO'S THERE?
DEWEY!
DEWEY **WHO?**
DEWEY HAVE TO GO THROUGH
THIS **EVERY** TIME I **KNOCK?**

KNOCK-KNOCK!
WHO'S THERE?

DIANE!

DIANE WHO?

DIANE TO MEET YOU!

YOE!

NOCK-KNOCK!
WHO'S THERE?
DORIS!
DORIS **WHO?**
DORIS OPEN -- CAN I
COME IN?

KNOCK-KNOCK!

WHO'S THERE?

DOUGLAS!

DOUGLAS **WHO**?

DOUGLAS IS HALF FULL!

KNOCK-KNOCK!
WHO'S THERE?
HYRAM!
HYRAM **WHO**?
HYRAM POPEYE THE SAILOR MAN!

Ding Dong!

What kind of door does a doctor have?
A sore door!

Knock-Knock!
Who's There?

DUSTIN!

DUSTIN WHO?

DUSTIN THE WIND!

KNOCK-KNOCK!
WHO'S THERE?
DUSTY!
DUSTY WHO?
DUSTY DOWN HERE -- BRING THE VACUUM!

Answer The Door!

What kind of door does a pig have?
A boar door!

NOCK-KNOCK!
WHO'S THERE?
GABE!
GABE **WHO?**
GABE ALL MY **MONEY** TO **CHARITY!**

KNOCK-KNOCK!
WHO'S THERE?
HAL!
HAL **WHO?**
HAL SHOULD I KNOW?

KNOCK-KNOCK!

WHO'S THERE?

JERRY!

JERRY WHO?

JERRY DOUGHNUTS ARE MY **FAVORITE!**

KNOCK-KNOCK!
WHO'S THERE?
GLADYS!
GLADYS **WHO?**
GLADYS ME, AREN'T YOU?

KNOCK-KNOCK!
WHO'S THERE?
HOLDEN!
HOLDEN **WHO?**
HOLDEN MY BREATH UNTIL YOU
LET ME IN!

KNOCK-KNOCK!
WHO'S THERE?
HELENE!
HELENE **WHO?**
HELENE-D OVER AND **KISSED ME!**

Ding Dong!

What kind of door does
a chiropractor have?
A back door!

KNOCK-KNOCK!

WHO'S THERE?

IRIS!

IRIS **WHO?**

IRIS-KED MY LIFE COMING OVER HERE!

HAR!

HAR!

KNOCK-KNOCK!
    WHO'S THERE?
IVANA!
    IVANA **WHO?**
IVANA COME IN!

NOCK-KNOCK!
WHO'S THERE?
JEWEL!
JEWEL **WHO?**
JEWEL LET ME IN IF YOU KNOW
WHAT'S **GOOD FOR YOU!**

**What number is on
Hamlet's apartment door?**
2-B (or not 2-B)!

Door Knobbies!

What note is on a whale's door?
I'll be humpback in 5 minutes!

KNOCK-KNOCK!

WHO'S THERE?

JONAH!

Chuckle!

JONAH WHO?

JONAH CAR OR LEASE ONE?

KNOCK-KNOCK!
WHO'S THERE?
JUDAH!
JUDAH WHO?
JUDAH MAN!

KNOCK-KNOCK!
WHO'S THERE?
JUDE!
JUDE **WHO?**
JUDE, WHERE'S MY CAR?

KNOCK-KNOCK!

WHO'S THERE?

CARL!

CARL **WHO?**

CARL STALL IF YOU **DON'T PUT GAS** IN IT!

KNOCK-KNOCK!
WHO'S THERE?
KEEGAN!
KEEGAN **WHO?**
A KEEGAN LET ME IN, YOU KNOW!

Knock-Knock!
Who's There?

LACEY!

LACEY WHO?

LACEY GOOD FOR NOTHING!

KNOCK-KNOCK!
WHO'S THERE?
KEISHA!
KEISHA **WHO?**
KEISHA WOULD **COME IN HANDY** RIGHT NOW!

 NOCK-KNOCK!
WHO'S THERE?
MACKENZIE!
MACKENZIE **WHO?**
**MACKENZIE EVERYTHING
YOU'RE DOING!**

 **Ding Dong!**

What does it sound
like when you knock on
Dr. Frankenstein's door?
"Shock! Shock!"

KNOCK-KNOCK!
WHO'S THERE?
MALCOLM!
MALCOLM **WHO?**
MALCOLMS FROM THE **POST OFFICE!**

KNOCK-KNOCK!

WHO'S THERE?

MARK!

MARK **WHO?**

MARK MY WORDS, I'LL BE BACK!

KNOCK-KNOCK!
WHO'S THERE?
KENT!
KENT **WHO?**
KENT REACH THE **DOORBELL** -- THAT'S WHY I'M **KNOCKING!**

NOCK-KNOCK!
WHO'S THERE?
MARTIAN!
MARTIAN **WHO?**
MARTIAN BAND!

KNOCK-KNOCK!

WHO'S THERE?

MARY LEE!

MARY LEE **WHO?**

MARY LEE, MARY LEE, MARY LEE, MARY LEE,
LIFE IS BUT A DREAM!

NOCK-KNOCK!
WHO'S THERE?
MACY!
MACY **WHO?**
MACY SOME ID?

 ## Door Knobbies!

What does it sound like when you
knock on a dressmaker's door?
"Frock! Frock!"

KNOCK-KNOCK!
WHO'S THERE?
NATHAN!
NATHAN **WHO?**
NATHAN NEW WITH ME; WHAT'
NEW WITH YOU?

What's the trick to walking through walls?
Using the door!

KNOCK-KNOCK!

WHO'S THERE?

NITA!

NITA **WHO?**

NITA KEY!

KNOCK-KNOCK!
WHO'S THERE?
NOAH!
NOAH **WHO?**
NOAH *GOOD RESTAURANT* AROUND HERE?

**K**NOCK-KNOCK!
      WHO'S THERE?
  ALBIE!
    ALBIE **WHO?**
ALBIE BACK!

KNOCK-KNOCK!
  WHO'S THERE?
AGATHA!
  AGATHA **WHO?**
AGATHA GO RIGHT NOW, I'LL **SEE YA LATER!**

KNOCK-KNOCK!
WHO'S THERE?
KRIS!
KRIS **WHO?**
KRIS-PY KREME DOUGHNUTS!

Knock-Knock!
Who's There?

C.D.!

C.D. WHO?

C.D. WORLD AND JOIN THE NAVY!

KNOCK-KNOCK!
WHO'S THERE?
RUSS!
RUSS **WHO?**
RUSS PILAF!

NOCK-KNOCK!
WHO'S THERE?
GORILLA!
GORILLA **WHO?**
GORILLA YOUR **DREAMS!**

 What did the man say
when he knocked on
the art museum door?
"Show me the Monet!"

 NOCK-KNOCK!
WHO'S THERE?
ETTA!
ETTA **WHO?**
ETTA SOMETHING THAT DIDN'T
AGREE WITH ME, I THINK I'M
GONNA **BARF!**

K NOCK-KNOCK!
        WHO'S THERE?
EUBIE!
        EUBIE **WHO?**
EUBIE-LONG IN A ZOO!

CAN YOU GET THAT ?
What did the horse say when
he knocked on the house next door?
"Good morning, neigh-bor!"

Ding Dong!

What do you call a
really cute door?
A-door-able!

KNOCK-KNOCK!

WHO'S THERE?

BERRY!

BERRY WHO?

BERRY NICE TO MEET YOU!

KNOCK-KNOCK!
WHO'S THERE?
NOAH!
NOAH WHO?
NOAH BUSINESS LIKE
SHOW BUSINESS!

KNOCK-KNOCK!

WHO'S THERE?

OLIVE!

OLIVE **WHO?**

OLIVE YOU! OPEN THE DOOR AND **GIVE ME A KISS!**

KNOCK-KNOCK!

WHO'S THERE?

NEWT!

NEWT **WHO?**

NEWT JERSEY IS THE **GARDEN STATE!**

KNOCK-KNOCK!

WHO'S THERE?

KANSAS!

KANSAS **WHO?**

KANSAS BE FRIDAY ALREADY?

DOOR SLAMS!

What color is Dracula's door?
Ghoul-den!

KNOCK-KNOCK!
WHO'S THERE?
MISSOURI!
MISSOURI WHO?
MISSOURI LOVES COMPANY!

NOCK-KNOCK!
WHO'S THERE?
MILO!
MILO **WHO?**
MILO-WER BACK ITCHES, PLEASE
SCRATCH IT!

Ding Dong!

What do you say when
Santa opens the door?
"Yo-ho ho ho!"

KNOCK-KNOCK!
   WHO'S THERE?
AGATHA!
   AGATHA **WHO?**
AGATHA GET OUT OF THIS PLACE!

KNOCK-KNOCK!
   WHO'S THERE?
JEN!
   JEN **WHO?**
**JEN IN ROME, DO AS
THE ROMANS DO!**

NOCK-KNOCK!
WHO'S THERE?
DENNY!
DENNY **WHO?**
DENNY BONE'S CONNECTED
TO THE **LEG BONE!**

KNOCK-KNOCK!

WHO'S THERE?

ALMA!

ALMA **WHO?**

ALMA THE ONE KNOCKING ON THE DOOR!

Knock-Knock!
Who's There?

CLAUDIA!

CLAUDIA **WHO**?

CLAUDIA DOCTOR, I'M SICK!

NOCK-KNOCK!
WHO'S THERE?
ALDA!
ALDA **WHO**?
ALDA PEOPLE IN THE **WORLD**
AND **YOU** HAD TO **ANSWER**
THE **DOOR**!

KNOCK-KNOCK!

WHO'S THERE?

YVETTE!

YVETTE **WHO?**

YVETTE MY PANTS!

KNOCK-KNOCK!
WHO'S THERE?
RILEY!
RILEY **WHO?**
RILEY COLD OUT HERE, LET ME IN!

What do you say when a florist opens the door?
"How's your mum?"

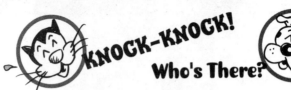

KNOCK-KNOCK!
  WHO'S THERE?
OZZIE!
  OZZIE WHO?
OZZIE YOUR HOUSE IS
FOR SALE!

KNOCK-KNOCK!
WHO'S THERE?
CELESTE!
CELESTE **WHO?**
CELESTE TIME I'M GONNA **TELL** YOU!

KNOCK-KNOCK!
WHO'S THERE?
TORI!
TORI **WHO?**
TORI BACK OF MY **PANTS** -- LET ME **IN!**

What do you say when a
dentist opens the door?
"How are you filling today?"

KNOCK-KNOCK!
WHO'S THERE?
PISA!
PISA WHO?
PISA CAKE!

KNOCK-KNOCK!
   WHO'S THERE?
BRINA!
   BRINA **WHO?**
BRINA KEY TO THE **DOOR!**

What do you say when
a teacher opens the door?
"You've got class!"

NOCK-KNOCK!
    WHO'S THERE?
ART!
    ART **WHO?**
ART FOR **ART'S SAKE!**

**K**NOCK-KNOCK!
WHO'S THERE?
HOWARD!
HOWARD **WHO?**
I'M FINE, **HOWARD YOU?**

CAN YOU GET THAT ❓
What do you say when
a foot doctor opens the door?
"Nice toe meet you!"

KNOCK-KNOCK!
WHO'S THERE?
PHIL!
PHIL **WHO?**
PHIL IT UP WITH **REGULAR!**

KNOCK-KNOCK!
WHO'S THERE?
GORILLA!
GORILLA **WHO?**
GORILLA SOME **HAMBURGERS!**

KNOCK-KNOCK!
  WHO'S THERE?
CARMEN!
  CARMEN **WHO?**
CARMEN TO MY **ARMS** AND
GIVE ME A **HUG!**

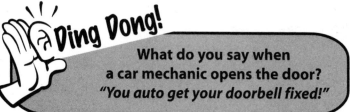

KNOCK-KNOCK!
WHO'S THERE?
IRIS!
IRIS **WHO?**
IRIS YOU WOULD **OPEN THE DOOR!**

KNOCK-KNOCK!
WHO'S THERE?
DENNIS!
DENNIS **WHO?**
DENNIS ANYONE?

KNOCK-KNOCK!
WHO'S THERE?
CARL!
CARL **WHO?**
CARL BE HERE TO **PICK US UP** SOON!

KNOCK-KNOCK!

WHO'S THERE?

YUKON!

YUKON **WHO?**

YUKON LEAD A **HORSE** TO **WATER,** BUT YOU **CAN'T** MAKE HIM **DRINK!**

KNOCK-KNOCK!
WHO'S THERE?
FERN!
FERN **WHO?**
FERN CRYING OUT LOUD, LET ME IN!

What sign does a car mechanic
have on his door?
No auto-body's home!

KNOCK-KNOCK!

WHO'S THERE?

NATHAN!

NATHAN **WHO?**

NATHAN BUT THE **BEST** FOR YOU!

KNOCK-KNOCK!
WHO'S THERE?
MARILYN!
MARILYN **WHO?**
MARILYN WE **ROLL** ALONG!

I-Screen, You-Screen!

What do you say when an optometrist opens the door?
"Nice to see you!"

KNOCK-KNOCK!

WHO'S THERE?

NOAH!

NOAH WHO?

NOAH PARKING ON THIS SIDE OF THE STREET!

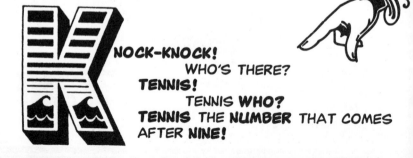

KNOCK-KNOCK!
WHO'S THERE?
TENNIS!
TENNIS WHO?
TENNIS THE NUMBER THAT COMES AFTER NINE!

KNOCK-KNOCK!
   WHO'S THERE?
TROY!
   TROY **WHO?**
TROY, TROY AGAIN!

KNOCK-KNOCK!
   WHO'S THERE?
CASHEW!
   CASHEW **WHO?**
CASHEW SEE I'M FREEZING OUT HERE?

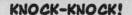

KNOCK-KNOCK!

WHO'S THERE?

CASSIUS!

CASSIUS **WHO?**

CASSIUS WHAT YOU NEED TO **BUY THINGS!**

DOOR SLAMS!

What do you say when
Dracula opens the door?
"Fangs for letting me in!"

KNOCK-KNOCK!
WHO'S THERE?
FUR!
FUR **WHO?**
FUR THE **LAST** TIME -- **OPEN** THE **DOOR!**

**K**NOCK-KNOCK!
WHO'S THERE?
INEZ!
INEZ **WHO?**
INEZ-ER ANSWER SUCH **STUPID QUESTIONS!**

NOCK-KNOCK!
  WHO'S THERE?
    ILENE!
  ILENE **WHO?**
    ILENE AGAINST THIS **DOOR** 'TIL
  YOU **OPEN UP!**

 Ding Dong!

What do you say when
you knock on a scale's door?
"I've been weighting here for hours!"

Knock-Knock!
Who's There?

ESTHER!

ESTHER WHO?

ESTHER BUNNY!

KNOCK-KNOCK!
    WHO'S THERE?
BUTCH!
    BUTCH **WHO?**
BUTCH YOUR **MONEY** WHERE
YOUR **MOUTH** IS!

**K**NOCK-KNOCK!
          WHO'S THERE?
DARRYL!
          DARRYL **WHO?**
DARRYL BE A **NEW MOON** TONIGHT!

**KNOCK-KNOCK!
WHO'S THERE?**

ISADORE!

ISADORE **WHO?**

ISADORE LOCKED?

**K**NOCK-KNOCK!
          WHO'S THERE?
DYLAN!
          DYLAN **WHO?**
DYLAN CARDS -- WANT
TO **PLAY** A **GAME?**

KNOCK-KNOCK!

WHO'S THERE?

JUSTICE!

JUSTICE WHO?

JUSTICE I SUSPECTED!

NOCK-KNOCK!
WHO'S THERE?
CHERI!
CHERI **WHO?**
CHERI-O, OLD CHAP!

Ding Dong!

What do you say when a computer geek opens the door?
"How's your rom?"

KNOCK-KNOCK!
WHO'S THERE?
COLLEEN!
COLLEEN **WHO?**
COLLEEN ALL **CARS!** **COLLEEN** ALL **CARS!**

KNOCK-KNOCK!
WHO'S THERE?
KAREN!
KAREN **WHO?**
KAREN HEAVY **BOXES** -- CAN YOU
OPEN THE **DOOR!**

KNOCK-KNOCK!
 WHO'S THERE?
LEIF!
 LEIF **WHO?**
LEIF ME **ALONE!**

KNOCK-KNOCK!

WHO'S THERE?

TRACEY!

TRACEY **WHO?**

TRACEY MY **STEPS** -- I LOST SOMETHING!

KNOCK-KNOCK!
WHO'S THERE?
ALLEN!
ALLEN **WHO?**
ALLEN-EED IS LOVE!

KNOCK-KNOCK!
WHO'S THERE?
PAT!
PAT **WHO?**
PAT THE **DOG** -- HE'S BRINGING IN THE **NEWSPAPER!**

Door Knobbies!

What do you say when
a cheerleader opens the door?
"How's your pom-pom?"

Knock-Knock!
Who's There?

ELLA!

ELLA **WHO?**

ELLA-LULLIA, SOMEONE'S **HOME!**

KNOCK-KNOCK!
WHO'S THERE?
PEARL!
PEARL **WHO?**
PEARL CHANCE I'LL **TELL** YOU IF
YOU **OPEN** THE **DOOR!**

 **NOCK-KNOCK!**
WHO'S THERE?
ALAN!
ALAN **WHO?**
ALAN YOU **TEN DOLLARS,** NOW
YOU'VE **GOT** TO PAY ME **BACK!**

KNOCK-KNOCK!
WHO'S THERE?
NEW YEAR!
NEW YEAR **WHO?**
NEW YEAR WERE GONNA **ASK** ME THAT!

What do you say when you
knock on a baker's door?
"Open sesame!"

KNOCK-KNOCK!
WHO'S THERE?
DONNA!
DONNA **WHO?**
DONNA EVER CHANGE; I LOVE
YOU **JUST** THE WAY YOU **ARE!**

JIMMY!

JIMMY **WHO?**

JIMMY A BREAK!

RNOCK-KNOCK!
WHO'S THERE?
RICH!
RICH **WHO?**
RICH WAY DID THEY **GO?**

KNOCK-KNOCK!

WHO'S THERE?

DANA!

DANA **WHO?**

DANA TALK TO ME LIKE **THAT!**

KNOCK-KNOCK!
WHO'S THERE?
DINAH!
DINAH **WHO?**
DINAH-SAUR!

Ding Dong!

What do you say when an antique dealer opens the door?
"What's new?"

Knock-Knock!
Who's There?

BONNIE!

BONNIE WHO?

BONNIE RABBIT!

NOCK-KNOCK!
WHO'S THERE?
CARRIE!
CARRIE **WHO?**
CARRIE ME BACK TO MY OLD VIRGINIA HOME!

Answer The Door!

What do you say when a buffalo opens the door? *"What's gnu?"*

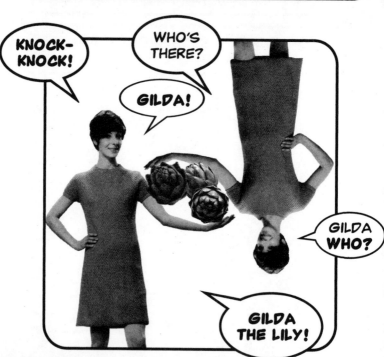

KNOCK-KNOCK!

WHO'S THERE?

GILDA!

GILDA WHO?

GILDA THE LILY!

KNOCK-KNOCK!
 WHO'S THERE?
CARLOS!
 CARLOS **WHO?**
CARLOS A **TIRE.**
DO YOU HAVE
A **SPARE?**

**K**NOCK-KNOCK!
WHO'S THERE?
HAZEL!
HAZEL **WHO?**
HAZEL-LONG, I'LL BE **SEEING** YOU!

KNOCK-KNOCK!
WHO'S THERE?
I'VE OFTEN **WONDERED** THAT **MYSELF...**

KNOCK-KNOCK!
　　　WHO'S THERE?
OPRAH!
　　　OPRAH **WHO?**
OPRAH THE **RIVER** AND **THROUGH THE WOODS**, TO **GRANDMOTHER'S HOUSE** WE **GO!**

KNOCK-KNOCK!
　　　WHO'S THERE?
ASHLEY!
　　　ASHLEY **WHO?**
ASHLEY, I DON'T REALLY **KNOW!**

NOCK-KNOCK!
WHO'S THERE?
AURORA!
AURORA WHO?
AURORA IS THE SOUND
A LION MAKES!

Ding Dong!
What does it sound like
when you knock on a bird's door?
"Hawk! Hawk!"

NOCK-KNOCK!
WHO'S THERE?
MERLE!
MERLE **WHO**?
MERLE, MERLE! IT'S YOUR
LITTLE **KITTY CAT**!

 NOCK-KNOCK!
     WHO'S THERE?
HUGO!
     HUGO **WHO?**
HUGO FLY A **KITE!**

What does a farmer use
to keep his door open?
A door crop!

Door Knobbies!

What does a housekeeper use
to keep her door open?
A door mop!

KNOCK-KNOCK!
WHO'S THERE?
TOUCAN!
TOUCAN **WHO?**
TOUCAN LIVE **CHEAPER** THAN **ONE!**

KNOCK-KNOCK!

WHO'S THERE?

FRANK LEE!

FRANK LEE **WHO?**

FRANK LEE, MY DEAR, I DON'T GIVE A DARN!

I-Screen, You-Screen!

What does a bunny use to keep her door open?
A door hop!

KNOCK-KNOCK!
WHO'S THERE?
THELMA!
THELMA **WHO?**
THELMA BOX IS FULL;
PICK UP YOUR **LETTERS!**

Knock-Knock!
Who's There?

KNOCK-KNOCK!
    WHO'S THERE?
BOB!
    BOB **WHO?**
BOB-ING FOR **APPLES!**

Ding Dong!

**What does a dad use
to keep his door open?**
A door pop!

KNOCK-KNOCK!
    WHO'S THERE?
THERESA!
    THERESA WHO?
THERESA NEW MOON RISING!

KNOCK-KNOCK!

WHO'S THERE?

PAULA!

PAULA WHO?

PAULA THE DOOR OPEN!

NOCK-KNOCK!
    WHO'S THERE?
    GERALD!
    GERALD WHO?
    GERALD GRANDPAPPY!

NOCK-KNOCK!
    WHO'S THERE?
MONTEL!
    MONTEL **WHO?**
MONTEL-EPHONE IS **RINGING,** AND
I'VE GOT TO **ANSWER** IT!

KNOCK-KNOCK!

WHO'S THERE?

JUSTIN!

JUSTIN **WHO?**

THIS JUSTIN . . . MAN BITES DOG!

NOCK-KNOCK!
WHO'S THERE?
IVANA!
IVANA **WHO?**
IVANA **COME IN!**

Door Knobbies!

What door does a comedian
knock on when he's sick?
The door to the he-he-mergency room!

KNOCK-KNOCK! WHO'S THERE?

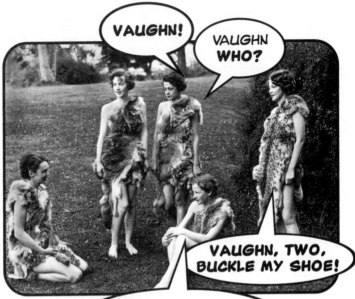

KNOCK-KNOCK!
WHO'S THERE?
NORA!
NORA WHO?
NORA WAY AM I GONNA TELL YOU!

I-Screen, You-Screen!

What does Jackie Chan use
to keep his door open?
A door chop!

KNOCK-KNOCK!

WHO'S THERE?

JIMMY!

JIMMY WHO?

JIMMY THE LOCK!

KNOCK-KNOCK!
WHO'S THERE?
LINDY!
LINDY WHO?
LINDY ME A CUP OF SUGAR, PLEASE!

KNOCK-KNOCK!

WHO'S THERE?

BAILEY!

BAILEY **WHO?**

BAILEY HEAR YA --
CAN YOU **SPEAK UP?**

YOE!

DOOR SLAMS!

What sound does an
ape's doorbell make?
"King Kong!"

KNOCK-KNOCK!
WHO'S THERE?
COLLIER!
COLLIER **WHO?**
COLLIER SISTER -- I'M HERE
FOR OUR **DATE!**

Knock-Knock!
Who's There?

LESLIE!

LESLIE **WHO?**

LESLIE THE DOOR **OPEN** NEXT TIME SO I CAN **WALK RIGHT IN!**

KNOCK-KNOCK!
WHO'S THERE?
EMMA!
EMMA **WHO?**
EMMA YANKEE DOODLE DANDY!

KNOCK-KNOCK!
WHO'S THERE?
FREDDIE!
FREDDIE WHO?
FREDDIE OR NOT, HERE I COME!

KNOCK-KNOCK!
WHO'S THERE?
MARIA!
MARIA **WHO?**
MARIA NAME IS **FLOOTERSNOOT**, BUT YOU CAN CALL ME **FLOOTIE!**

What sound does a music teacher's doorbell make?
"Sing Song!"

NOCK-KNOCK!
WHO'S THERE?
MORGAN!
MORGAN WHO?
MORGAN YOU CAN HANDLE --
I BROUGHT THE WHOLE FAMILY!

KNOCK-KNOCK!
WHO'S THERE?
SHELBY!
SHELBY **WHO?**
SHELBY COMIN' AROUND THE
MOUNTAIN WHEN SHE **COMES!**

KNOCK-KNOCK!
    WHO'S THERE?
NORM!
    NORM **WHO?**
NORM-ALLY THESE JOKES
ARE **MUCH FUNNIER** THAN THIS!

CAN YOU GET THAT ?

What sound does a table-tennis
player's doorbell make?
"Ping Pong!"

Ding Dong!

What sound does a
bee's doorbell make?
"Sting Stong!"

KNOCK-
KNOCK!

WHO'S
THERE?

OWLS
GO!

OWLS GO
WHO?

THAT'S
RIGHT,
THEY **DO!**

KNOCK-KNOCK!
    WHO'S THERE?
SAMANTHA!
    SAMANTHA **WHO?**
SAMANTHA SEE ABOUT
THE **PLUMBING!**

KNOCK-KNOCK!
WHO'S THERE?
GRACE!
GRACE **WHO?**
GRACE ME WITH YOUR **PRESENCE**, WILL YOU?

KNOCK-KNOCK!
WHO'S THERE?
JUSTIN!
JUSTIN **WHO?**
JUSTIN CASE!

K NOCK-KNOCK!
WHO'S THERE?
AMANDA!
AMANDA **WHO?**
AMANDA HUG AND **KISS!**

KNOCK-KNOCK!
WHO'S THERE?
BRUCE!
BRUCE **WHO?**
I **BRUCE** SOME **TEA** AND BROUGHT IT **OVER!**

KNOCK-KNOCK!
WHO'S THERE?
IDA!
IDA **WHO?**
IDA KNOW!

NOCK-KNOCK!
WHO'S THERE?
MYA!
MYA **WHO?**
MYA **SUGAR BOWL** IS **EMPTY** --
CAN I **BORROW** A CUP?

KNOCK-KNOCK!

WHO'S THERE?

MAJOR!

MAJOR **WHO?**

MAJOR LOOK!

  KNOCK-KNOCK!
WHO'S THERE?
NOAH!
NOAH **WHO?**
NOAH THYSELF!

 What are most doors made of?
Wood-n't you like to know?

KNOCK-KNOCK!

WHO'S THERE?

LITTLE OLD LADY!

LITTLE OLD LADY **WHO?**

I DIDN'T KNOW YOU COULD **YODEL!**

YOE!

KNOCK-KNOCK!
WHO'S THERE?
OLIVIA!
OLIVIA **WHO?**
OLIVIA ME ALONE!

What is a thief's door made of?
Steel!

KNOCK-KNOCK!

WHO'S THERE?

ROSE!

ROSE WHO?

ROSE THE BEEF, I'M HUNGRY!

KNOCK-KNOCK!
WHO'S THERE?
EDDIE!
EDDIE WHO?
EDDIE-BODY HOME?

KNOCK-KNOCK!
WHO'S THERE?
DISGUISE!
DISGUISE **WHO?**
DISGUISE ARE **CLOUDY;**
CAN I BORROW YOUR **UMBRELLA?**

KNOCK-KNOCK!
WHO'S THERE?
ORANGE!
ORANGE **WHO?**
ORANGE YOU GOING TO LET ME **IN?**

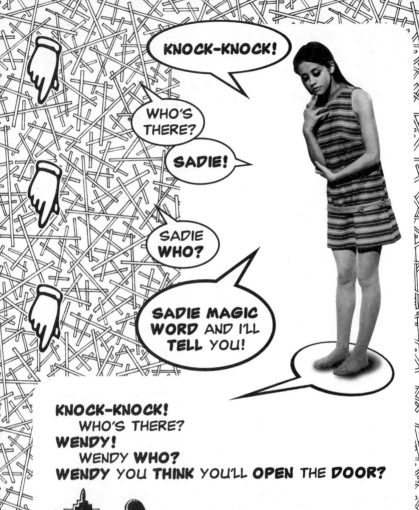

KNOCK-KNOCK!
 WHO'S THERE?
WENDY!
 WENDY **WHO?**
WENDY YOU **THINK** YOU'LL **OPEN** THE **DOOR?**

NOCK-KNOCK!
 WHO'S THERE?
 IGOR!
 IGOR **WHO?**
IGOR TO **TALK** TO YOU!
LET ME **IN!**

NOCK-KNOCK!
WHO'S THERE?
PITCHER!
PITCHER **WHO?**
PITCHER ARMS AROUND ME!

KNOCK-KNOCK!
WHO'S THERE?
JAMAICA!
JAMAICA **WHO?**
JAMAICA ME **SICK!**

NOCK-KNOCK!
WHO'S THERE?
THERMOS!
THERMOS **WHO?**
THERMOS BE A **REASON** YOU
WON'T LET ME IN, BUT I **CAN'T**
FIGURE IT **OUT!**

What looks like a door,
feels like a door,
and smells like a door?
A door!

 NOCK-KNOCK!
WHO'S THERE?
MARCELLA!
MARCELLA **WHO?**
MARCELLA IS AT THE **BOTTOM**
OF MY **HOUSE!**

KNOCK-KNOCK!
WHO'S THERE?
ZANY!
ZANY **WHO?**
ZANY-BODY IN **THERE?**

KNOCK-KNOCK!
    WHO'S THERE?
YACHT!
    YACHT **WHO?**
YACHT NOT ASK SO
MANY **QUESTIONS!**

CAN YOU GET THAT?

What begins with D, ends with R, and makes a knocking sound?
A drummer!

Ding Dong!

What day will a chicken
not open his door?
Fry-day!

KNOCK-KNOCK!

WHO'S THERE?

TAMARA!

TAMARA WHO?

TAMARA IS ANOTHER DAY!

NOCK-KNOCK!
WHO'S THERE?
ALMA!
ALMA WHO?
ALMA WOMAN OF MYSTERY!

KNOCK-KNOCK!
> WHO'S THERE?

XAVIER!
> XAVIER **WHO?**

XAVIER BREATH; I WON'T
ANSWER YOUR **QUESTIONS!**

KNOCK-KNOCK!
> WHO'S THERE?

NICHOLAS!
> NICHOLAS **WHO?**

NICHOLAS FOUR CENTS MORE THAN A **PENNY!**

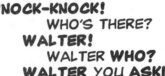

KNOCK-KNOCK!
  WHO'S THERE?
ICY!
  ICY WHO?
ICY NO REASON FOR NOT
LETTING ME IN!

Ding Dong!

What does it sound like
when you knock on a seagull's door?
"Flock! Flock!"

**K**NOCK-KNOCK!
    WHO'S THERE?
TERESE!
    TERESE **WHO?**
TERESE A **REASON** YOU'RE NOT LETTING
ME IN, BUT I **DON'T KNOW** WHAT IT **IS!**

KNOCK-KNOCK!

WHO'S THERE?

TRIXIE!

TRIXIE **WHO?**

TRIXIES ARE FOR **KIDSIES!**

KNOCK-KNOCK!
    WHO'S THERE?
AARON!
    AARON **WHO?**
AARON THE **SIDE** OF **CAUTION!**

What day do you open
your door twice?
Two-sday!

KNOCK-KNOCK!
        WHO'S THERE?
ATTILA!
        ATTILA **WHO?**
ATTILA YOUR **MOTHER** IF YOU
DON'T LET ME **IN!**

NOCK-KNOCK!
WHO'S THERE?
WARNER!
WARNER **WHO?**
WARNER GO TO A **MOVIE**
WITH ME?

KNOCK-KNOCK!
WHO'S THERE?
WILDA!
WILDA **WHO?**
WILDA LADY OF THE **HOUSE**
PLEASE LET ME **IN?**

KNOCK-KNOCK!
WHO'S THERE?
FIFI!
FIFI **WHO?**
FIFI, FIE FIE, FO FO, FUM FUM!

NOCK-KNOCK!
WHO'S THERE?
LEDA!
LEDA **WHO**?
LEDA **HORSE** TO **WATER**,
BUT YOU **CAN'T** MAKE IT **DRINK**!

KNOCK-KNOCK!
WHO'S THERE?
ANNAPOLIS!
ANNAPOLIS **WHO**?
ANNAPOLIS **DAY** KEEPS THE **DOCTOR** AWAY!

 NOCK-KNOCK!
WHO'S THERE?
SWEEPIE!
SWEEPIE **WHO**?
SWEEPIE UNDER THE **RUGGIE**!

 MAC!

MAC **WHO**?

 MAC A **FUSS**!

YOE!

 NOCK-KNOCK!
WHO'S THERE?
DON!
DON **WHO**?
DON QUIT YOUR
DAY JOB!

NOCK-KNOCK!
WHO'S THERE?
MAMA!
MAMA WHO?
MAMA SAID THERE'D BE
DAYS LIKE THIS!

Ding Dong!

What kind of door
did Elvis have?
A pompa-door!

Knock-Knock!
Who's There?

COLE!

COLE WHO?

COLE YOUR MOTHER!

NOCK-KNOCK!
WHO'S THERE?
COUNT!
COUNT WHO?
COUNT-ING THE MINUTES!

NOCK-KNOCK!
WHO'S THERE?
CAIN!
CAIN **WHO**?
CAIN OF **WORMS**!

KNOCK-KNOCK!
WHO'S THERE?

AL!

AL **WHO**?

AL-PHABET SOUP!

NOCK-KNOCK!
WHO'S THERE?
STAN!
STAN **WHO**?
STAN PAT!

KNOCK-KNOCK!
   WHO'S THERE?
GRANT!
   GRANT **WHO?**
GRANT AND **BEAR** IT!

KNOCK-KNOCK!

WHO'S THERE?

DUANE!

DUANE **WHO?**

DUANE THE BATHTUB -- I'M **DWOWNING!**

 NOCK-KNOCK!
WHO'S THERE?
DALE!
DALE WHO?
DALE ME IN!

Door Knobbies!

What kind of door
does a cheater have?
A scheme door!

Knock-Knock!
Who's There?

RHEA!

RHEA WHO?

RHEA MY LIPS!

KNOCK-KNOCK!
WHO'S THERE?
PAUL!
PAUL WHO?
PAUL YOURSELF UP
BY YOUR BOOTSTRAPS!

I-Screen, You-Screen!

What kind of door does a dry cleaner have?
A steam door!

KNOCK-KNOCK!

WHO'S THERE?

DAWN!

DAWN WHO?

DAWN WORRY, BE HAPPY!

NOCK-KNOCK!
WHO'S THERE?
DOUGHNUT!
DOUGHNUT **WHO?**
DOUGHNUT BE YOUR
OWN WORST ENEMY!

KNOCK-KNOCK!
  WHO'S THERE?
WAYNE!
  WAYNE **WHO?**
WAYNE THE **GOING GETS TOUGH,**
THE **TOUGH GET GOING!**

KNOCK-KNOCK!
  WHO'S THERE?
WAYNE!
  WAYNE **WHO?**
WAYNE LIFE GIVES YOU **LEMONS,**
MAKE **LEMONADE!**

KNOCK-KNOCK!
 WHO'S THERE?
SUE!
 SUE WHO?
SUE ME!

KNOCK-KNOCK! WHO'S THERE?

STU!

STU WHO?

IF THE STU FITS, WEAR IT!

KNOCK-KNOCK!
 WHO'S THERE?
RAY!
 RAY WHO?
RAY-SE THE ROOF!

NOCK-KNOCK!
WHO'S THERE?
MAURA!
MAURA WHO?
MAURA THE MERRIER!

What kind of door
does a living room have?
A TV screen door!

Knock-Knock!
Who's There?

FRAN!

FRAN **WHO?**

FRAN IN NEED IS A FRAN INDEED!

NOCK-KNOCK!
WHO'S THERE?
FRITZ!
FRITZ **WHO?**
FRITZ TO BE **TIED!**

Answer The Door!

What kind of door is on a haunted house? *A scream door!*

NOCK-KNOCK!
WHO'S THERE?
GRANNY!
GRANNY **WHO?**
GRANNY ME A **MINUTE** OF YOUR **TIME!**

NOCK-KNOCK!
WHO'S THERE?
HEDDA!
HEDDA **WHO?**
HEDDA THE **PACK!**

NOCK-KNOCK!
WHO'S THERE?
HEDDA!
HEDDA **WHO?**
HEDDA HURTS --
HAVE-A AN ASPIRIN?

KNOCK-KNOCK!

WHO'S THERE?

FRITZ!

FRITZ **WHO?**

YOUR **REFRIGERATOR** IS ON THE **FRITZ!** HELP!

CAN YOU GET THAT ?

What does a beaver's mom tell him when he goes out? *"Don't dam the door!"*

KNOCK-KNOCK!
WHO'S THERE?
KEN!
KEN **WHO?**
KEN I COME IN?!

KNOCK-KNOCK!
WHO'S THERE?
NOAH!
NOAH **WHO?**
NOAH PROBLEM!

NOCK-KNOCK!
WHO'S THERE?
VERA!
VERA **WHO?**
VERA WHERE HAS MY
LITTLE DOG GONE?

 Ding Dong!

What does a goat's mom
tell him when he goes out?
"Don't ram the door!"

NOCK-KNOCK!
WHO'S THERE?
DON TOOTIE!
DON TOOTIE **WHO?**
DON TOOTIE YOUR OWN **HORN!**

KNOCK-KNOCK!
WHO'S THERE?
SOL!
SOL **WHO?**
THAT'S SOL, FOLKS!

What does a sweet potato's mom
tell her when she goes out?
"Don't yam the door!"

KNOCK-KNOCK!
WHO'S THERE?
NATHAN!
NATHAN **WHO**?
NATHAN DOING!

KNOCK-KNOCK!
WHO'S THERE?
STU!
STU **WHO**?
STU-DENT DRIVER!

I-Screen, You-Screen!

What does a shellfish's mom tell him
when he goes out?
"Don't clam the door!"

KNOCK-KNOCK!
WHO'S THERE?
LAURA!
LAURA **WHO?**
LAURA YOUR **MUSIC** -- YOU'RE
KEEPING ME **AWAKE!**

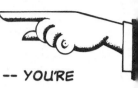

Knock-Knock!
Who's There?

**NOCK-KNOCK!**
WHO'S THERE?
DENISE!
DENISE **WHO?**
DENISE AND **DENEPHEW!**

What does a jelly donut's mom tell her when she goes out?
"Don't jam the door!"

NOCK-KNOCK!
WHO'S THERE?
HOLLY!
HOLLY **WHO?**
HOLLY-WEEN!

KNOCK-KNOCK!

WHO'S THERE?

PANCHO!

PANCHO **WHO?**

PANCHO LIGHTS OUT IF YOU DON'T
LET ME **IN!**

K NOCK-KNOCK!
WHO'S THERE?
PEEPHOLE!
PEEPHOLE **WHO?**
PEEPHOLE WHO LIVE IN
GLASS HOUSES
SHOULDN'T THROW **STONES!**

Door Knobbies!

What does a sheep's mom tell him
when he goes out?
"Don't lamb the door!"

KNOCK-KNOCK!
  WHO'S THERE?
FELON!
  FELON **WHO?**
FELON THE **ICE** -- YOU'LL HEAR
FROM MY **LAWYER!**

I-Screen, You-Screen!

What do you say when the doorbell doesn't smell?
"The doorbell is out of odor!"

 NOCK-KNOCK!
WHO'S THERE?
POLO!
POLO **WHO?**
POLO THE **LEADER!**

**K**NOCK-KNOCK!

WHO'S THERE?

MISTY!

MISTY **WHO?**

MISTY BUS -- GIVE ME A RIDE!

KNOCK-KNOCK!

WHO'S THERE?

REDFORD!

REDFORD **WHO?**

REDFORD IS PARKED BEHIND MY **CAR;** CAN YOU **MOVE** IT?

KNOCK-KNOCK!

WHO'S THERE?

SAWYER!

SAWYER **WHO?**

SAWYER IN HALF -- I'M A **MAGICIAN!**

DOOR SLAMS!

What do you call it when you hang a coat on the door?
Clothes-ing the door!

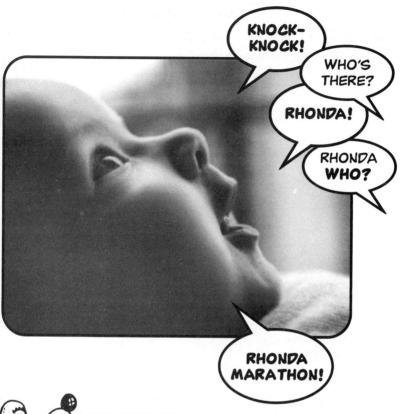

NOCK-KNOCK!
 WHO'S THERE?
ROCCO 'N' ROLLO!
 ROCCO 'N' ROLLO **WHO?**
ROCCO 'N' ROLLO IS HERE TO **STAY!**

What do you call it when
you insult a door?
Slamming the door!

NOCK-KNOCK!
WHO'S THERE?
ROB AND RUTH!
ROB AND RUTH WHO?
RUTH LEFT -- NOW IT'S JUST
ME, ROB. I'M RUTH-LESS!

KNOCK-KNOCK!
WHO'S THERE?
OLIVER!
OLIVER **WHO?**
OLIVER SUDDEN
I CAN'T **REMEMBER!**

KNOCK-KNOCK!
WHO'S THERE?
SADIE!
SADIE **WHO?**
SADIE MAGIC WORD!

CAN YOU GET THAT?

What do you call
a bullfighter's door?
A mata-door!

Ding Dong!

What do you do on a baby's doormat?
Diaper your feet!

KNOCK-KNOCK!

WHO'S THERE?

CLARA!

CLARA **WHO?**

CLARA-NET IS WHAT I **PLAY** IN THE **BAND!**

KNOCK-KNOCK!
WHO'S THERE?
PIANO!
PIANO **WHO?**
PIANO FLOOR IF YOU DON'T **LET ME IN!**

KNOCK-KNOCK!
  WHO'S THERE?
WALKER!
  WALKER **WHO?**
WALKER RUN -- WHICH
SHOULD WE DO?

KNOCK-KNOCK!
  WHO'S THERE?
ABBOTT!
  ABBOTT **WHO?**
ABBOTT TIME YOU **OPENED** THE **DOOR!**

KNOCK-KNOCK!

WHO'S THERE?

IMA!

IMA **WHO?**

IMA **HERE** TO **PICK UP** YOUR **DAUGHTER!**

DOOR SLAMS!

What do you do on a computer's doormat?
"Type your feet!"

NOCK-KNOCK!
    WHO'S THERE?
SCOLD!
    SCOLD WHO?
SCOLD AT THE NORTH POLE!

NOCK-KNOCK!
WHO'S THERE?
ANVIL!
ANVIL **WHO?**
ANVIL YOU TELL ME **YOUR** NAME, **TOO?**

What do you do on an apple's doormat?
Ripe your feet!

KNOCK-KNOCK!
WHO'S THERE?
CEREAL!
CEREAL **WHO?**
CEREAL PLEASURE TO **MEET** YOU!

KNOCK-KNOCK!

WHO'S THERE?

BERTHA!

BERTHA **WHO?**

BERTHA A NATION!

KNOCK-KNOCK!

WHO'S THERE?

DINAH!

DINAH WHO?

DINAH'S READY, WASH UP!

KNOCK-KNOCK!
 WHO'S THERE?
CHEESE!
 CHEESE **WHO?**
CHEESE THE **GIRL**
OF MY **DREAMS!**

What do you do on
a plumber's doormat?
Pipe your feet!

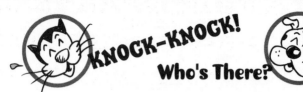

KNOCK-KNOCK!
Who's There?

NOCK-KNOCK!
WHO'S THERE?
PIGS!
PIGS WHO?
NO, OWLS WHO; PIGS OINK!

I-Screen, You-Screen!

What do you do on a public relations executive's doormat?
Hype your feet!

KNOCK-KNOCK!
WHO'S THERE?
GWEN!
GWEN **WHO?**
GWEN THE **MOON** HITS YOUR
EYE LIKE A BIG **PIZZA PIE** . . .

KNOCK-KNOCK!
WHO'S THERE?
ETHAN!
ETHAN **WHO?**
ETHAN AN **APPLE** A **DAY**
KEEPS THE **DOCTOR AWAY!**

KNOCK-KNOCK!
   WHO'S THERE?
MEGAN!
   MEGAN **WHO?**
MEGAN A **LIST,** CHECKIN' IT **TWICE!**

Knock-Knock!
Who's There?

HERA!

HERA **WHO?**

HERA COMES THE **BRIDE!**

YOE!

**KNOCK-KNOCK!**
   WHO'S THERE?
HIPPIE!
   HIPPIE **WHO?**
HIPPIE MEAL!

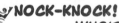

KNOCK-KNOCK!
WHO'S THERE?
JENNY!
JENNY **WHO?**
JENNY OLD THING WILL **DO!**

What does it sound like when
you knock on a
traffic signal's door?
"Walk! Walk!"

KNOCK-KNOCK!
WHO'S THERE?
SAM!
SAM **WHO?**
SAM PERSON WHO WAS
KNOCKING **A MINUTE AGO!**

KNOCK-KNOCK!

WHO'S THERE?

KETCHUP!

KETCHUP **WHO?**

KETCHUP ON **ALL** THE LATEST **GOSSIP!**

KNOCK-KNOCK!
   WHO'S THERE?
KIP!
   KIP **WHO?**
KIP YOUR **EYES** ON YOUR **OWN** PAPER!

 NOCK-KNOCK!
WHO'S THERE?
BESS!
BESS WHO?
BESS PERSONALITY!

CAN YOU GET THAT ?

What does it sound like when
you knock on a locksmith's door?
"Lock! Lock!"

Ding Dong!

What does it sound like when you knock on a parrot's door?
"Talk! Talk!"

NOCK-KNOCK!
WHO'S THERE?
STEVEN!
STEVEN **WHO?**
STEVEN I DON'T KNOW THE ANSWER TO **THAT** ONE!

KNOCK-KNOCK!

WHO'S THERE?

WANDA!

WANDA **WHO?**

WANDA GO TO THE **MOVIES?**

KNOCK-KNOCK!
WHO'S THERE?
YOGURT!
YOGURT **WHO?**
YOGURT YOUR WAY, AND I'LL GO **MINE!**

Ding Dong!

What does it sound like
when you knock on a boat's door?
"Dock! Dock!"

DOOR JAM

What does it sound like when
you knock on a foot's door?
"Sock! Sock!"

KNOCK-KNOCK!
WHO'S THERE?
YOUR MOM!
YOUR MOM **WHO?**
VERY FUNNY, NOW LET ME **IN!**